I Have Fallen *in* Love
with the World
and other poems

by

Tracey Schmidt

Schmidt, Tracey.
I Have Fallen in Love with the World: The Poetry of Tracey Schmidt
ISBN-13: 978-0-9815757-1-1

Cover design and photography by Tracey Schmidt
Border detail from the Late Shahjahan Album,
courtesy of the Sackler Gallery/Smithsonian Institute.

Logosophia Books
Mars Hill, NC
www.logosophiabooks.com

Contents

All poetry is prayer.

IRISH SAYING

I have fallen in love with the world....

The Poetry of Tracey Schmidt

Effulgence

Effulgence

All winter long
I tried and tried
To find a way
Through your sloped frown
And terse eyes

I never knew how
To please you.
Though in my
Uncomfortable heart
I yearned for your
Joy
And exclusive hand

It is lonely knowing you.

But one day
I understood
The barren judgment
You inhabit.

Nothing
Enough

No deep reservoir of
Care
In which to dip.
And so
I learned to
Love my own
Benevolent landscape
And drink
From my own
Effulgent
Cupped hands.
The inherited
Disapproving clutch
Opened
Releasing
A radiant drop of
Freedom.

Wash The Mud Away

I remember
Being a child
Careful
Lest I reveal
The real me–
Old, been-here-long-time woman
Trapped in a child's body.
Silent.
Afraid of awakening
Their fear or disbelief
Or jealousy.

And so we grow to be adults
Hiding our jewels in
The mudbasket.
Maybe,
When future days come,
We'll reach for the stars
And pluck
Enough
Courage

Down from the sky
To light up
The whole stream
And wash
The
Mud
Away.

Grief

Grief- my tag-along, noble friend
Grief that I was born with.
Brought from the tombs of Cairo
Smuggled in from Las Crucas.
Nurtured into being on a reservation.
Grief, my wrenching, alcoholic family-father-sister
story.
I need you no more.
You have served me well.
Remembered my birthdays and Christmas—
Been there late at night.
I don't know why I've outgrown your
Ashen, lonely colors.
Your pursed, down turned lips
Your empty house, blood red and rageful.
Rageful into the dusk and dawn of chained existence.
You serve me no more.
Go.
Go and find your peace
Elsewhere.
This
Heart
Is
Birthing
Love.

A Tree Has Fallen in the Woods

The lumberjacks inside of me heard
A tree fall in the woods yesterday.
And yes, by the way,
I was there to hear it….
The 'whump' felt in the ground
Of my still heart,
Where I have been treading a lot lately
Felt so immeasurably sure of its meaning-
The sound of something
Dying
In a place whistling with life,
That I rounded them up
And sent them out
To frantically dig
With their axes
A small soft space
for
Seeded newness
And to whisper, deep into the hole,
"Forgive me."

Enough

She dreamed
Of the day she would have
Enough courage
To drop her idea
Of the way it
Should be.
Then, she would step
Into the wild pool
And bathe into the
Joy
that only
This letting go
Could bring.
When her heart asked her,
"When will this be?"
She ran a thousand miles
Away
And finally over her shoulder looked
To see if it followed.

We throw bricks at our heart,
As if we could break that love.
And when we finally hold
Our own hand,
And say to that mirror image
"You, so beautiful
So beautiful."
Our hearts will shine
And we will find
That courage
Was enough

Was enough
All along.

Jealousy

Jealousy,
A forget-me-not
Poison—
Seeps into the ground
Like blood,
Ravages our peace
Like temptresses.
And for what?

If we do not
Have what we need,
And do not
Believe
We can call it forth—
Then
Perhaps
It was not really
Ours in the first place

And the
Anointing
Of
Trust

Into that hollow emptiness

Is
All
That we
Thirsted For
All
Along.

Claire's Family Kitchen

Dirt on floor—
Grit so thick you could hear it.
We loved to cook when
We were little
French Castles in
Vanilla icing- in 6th grade
Once we made a quilt
Of scraps our mothers had—
We thought we were grandmothers.
Her dog so big
We rode him through the house like a horse.
I always thought,
If all else fails,
I'll become large and dimpled
And make divine food.
No kitchen,
Even this one,
Too small to hold
The magic
Of the word
Everyone.

Slouch

If our body is a vessel
Slouch
Is to leave mud on the rooftop
And trash at the door.
Altar of Bone and Heart
A carriage of the mirror
Known to us
By that little word,
God.
Simple in its Mystery—
Given completely
Even
To this 5'9" vessel
Called Life.

Secret Lodges

There are Secret Lodges
In our Body-
Hard, Isolated, Tense.
Like a permanent Ruin
From an Unresolved
Fight
Or
From Arrows
Spit Out
In an Insult or Betrayal.

Formed in the Mouth
Like Stakes-
Driven
Into your Cells,
Like an invisible, stagnant memory.

Take Them out Now.
Watch the Pierced Body Heal over
And Fill.
Anointed.
Let the new Skin
Become Ground
For the running Deer
Who have been Forever Seeking
Your Open, Welcoming Field.

Roof Line

When I was young
I would lie in bed
Watching the sky-ceiling
Knowing

There were a hundred worlds up there–
Where we all come from.
And I would silently speak, saying:
I know You are busy with

Wars and famines and presidents and kings
But if you could come and take me to my people–

I would be very appreciative.
I knew by the way the
Stars circled and swirled
I was heard.

And one day,
Family
Would appear.
Like a ring.

Like a window
Into Love.
And I would be sitting
On the inside, looking out,

Instead of how I am now—
Under the star canopy
Wondering
When the roof line will appear.

It's Me

"It's me,"
I said.
But the Beloved
Cried and cried
Until I relented
And now I see
It's
Us
Who created
This poem.
This memory box
Which holds
Love jewels for the
Beloved and my heart.
We dance on the page now-
He turns the pages,
A twinkle in his eye,
I make coffee
For our break.

And so it goes,
This broken heart,
Like a rock split in two
Waiting for the Beloved to repair
And to write on.

* Beloved is a term often used in Sufi poetry
to refer to God.

Wild Spirits

The wild spirits outside
Are looking in my window—
Like a prayer, kneeling
Relieved that I am listening.

We run at lightning speed
Our lives loud – not like thunder,
But like the powerless rumble of fear
yapping
At the quiet intruder at the window.

Our longing
To see, to hear, to feel,
Never deeper than this moment–
Will never leave us.

The garden of our pain
Is nothing
Compared to our
Terrified flights.
Listen.
Can you hear it?

The wild spirits outside
Are trying to come in.

Deep Stillness

In the deep stillness of the night
When the moon takes over
The sky
And the stars come out
To ecstatically dance,
When the angelic beings curl up inside soft
Moss-laden swirls
And slumber—
Listen
To the ebb and flow
Of that pulsing, sacred song—
The one that is in great concert
With every
Peaceful hum—
And calls
To God
For the score.
And feels grace cradled
In the quiet, rhythmic base line.

Inside
That silent joy
Know
That
Great love
Rises up in between the notes
To fill
Every tiny cell
Every waiting vessel
Every
Moist, beating heart.

A Petition

I have often pondered
Your plan
To test us until we are completely soaked
In our tears and sweat—
Your vision to temper us
Into swords of light
Must be perfect and wise.
But at the moment
I cannot even find my sheath.

The magnificent world
You have created
Completely drenched in grief and despair
Has found unspeakable joy
Ready to be birthed
Into a thousand worlds–
Sitting under my tongue.

If I open my mouth
They will fly out, uncensored,
And ignite a holy fire–

Transforming
Silent aching
Into moist, fertile
Brilliance.

Lock the Door

"Lock the Door,"
She said.
But the Fox at my heart
Said
" Open"
And I did.
Now, myriad tracks
Walk in and celebrate
The Wolf, the Bear,
The tiny Spider.
And all I know
To say,
Is
" Welcome"
Welcome to the
Unlocked door
At the edge
Of
This state
That has no name
Where the signs,
Everywhere,
Read,
"Step right in."

I Cannot Make Myself Small

I cannot make myself small for you
I cannot reduce the layers of expression,
Nor shrink from
The large thoughts in my mouth.

Would a flower refusing to bloom
Make the world any more beautiful?

We drink from the same bottle,
Each cool sip washing down into the earth like rain.
No where do we feel this more
Than when we take the lid off
And let the thirst-quenching thunder run down our
chins—
The stains on our chests
War wounds
Of a life
Fully
Drunk
Up.

Fruits of Forgetfulness

When offered the fruit of
Forgetfulness
We are all offered
Upon entrance,
I declined.

Favoring instead
The messy recognition
Of my past:
Jaguar, Hunter
Queen, Servant, Motherless Child.
The ancient clock
In our faces
Repeating the story
Again and again.

And
Love is the secret language
That cracks the shell
And invites God in,
So that
One day

We may find ourselves
Traversing
Down the chute of our being
To that persistent
Holy
Place
Called
Oneness.

It's In the Silence

It's in the quiet moments
Our life speaks most loudly—
In between the cracks
Of our shouting
And
Our mystical need to
Run like hell
From ourselves.

And when
The Coin of the Realm,
Stillness,

Finally breaks through
And invites us
To embrace ourselves,
Judgment and conditions left behind—
The need breaks wide open
And all the paths
Rush at breakneck speed

To this
Moment.

To
This moment
Of
Love.

A Tear from His Dream

In my dream I am running to catch up
To what God
Has given me.
Or maybe it was just a
Tear dropped from His dream
That I caught in mid-air.
Now,
Cradled in my hands
Like a drop of nectar
Sinking into my skin,
I listen to
That silent amalgam.
It is both a curse and a blessing
To be an artist.
To hear a vision
Say, "Give me a voice."
I open its mouth
In hopes that I can
Answer that tear
And silently mop up the stream.

Cavernous Star-Studded Mouth

The whole world could swallow me up.
Not swallow me up and spit me out,
But swallow me up and
Hold me
In that nurturing radiance
Of spoken and unspoken power.
Like being held in the cavernous star-studded mouth
of the sky,
Ready to sing light out everywhere.

Shrapnel

Bloodbaths
Are started this way:
A hurt glance,
An unresolved tear—
Brittle shards
Called, collectively,
"Me."

We know that me:
Arrogant, terrified, broken.

Some things are battle worthy.
Most, a trifle born of
Shrapnel
We succumbed to,
Left in our festering, grasping hand.

When spring comes
The beaks will lift up
Those tiny bits of straw called
Jealousy, fear,

And form them, bit by bit, into
Vessels
Which hold eggs
That quietly yell, "Wake Up."

Bloodbath?
What bloodbath?
All I see are the
Nests
At
My
Doorstep.

Churning

When
The shouting heart
Is finally heard
Amidst the rubble—
So that its
Whisper is
The only background noise—

When
The jagged edges of
Thought and fear are
Worn down to mirrored stone,

Something happens
To that ocean
Inside of us—

All the churning gives way.

And the glassy surface
Teems with creative fish
That come out to
Mate and jump
And play–

Announcing
The presence
Of every ocean in the world
Reflecting off of
That
One
Shining
Glistening
Surface.

Ally

Either
You are an ally
Or not.

Either you are carrying forward
The great work of
Bringing love into the world,

Or you feel your heart crumble like black bark–
Decaying on the pungent forest floor.
Scarified into the dark, cleansing earth.

Either the heat of light
Melts our hot-house plant ideas of right and wrong,
Sprung up from fierce reason,

Or the wild cup cools our rabid tongue
And insistent thoughts
Which keep the heart

Busy from its
Razor-sharp work
Of carrying forward
The great work
Of love.

I Have Fallen in

I have fallen in love with the world.
I'm not exactly sure when it happened—
It wasn't on the first date
It wasn't even on the
Ten thousandth.
First, we had to become friends
That in itself
Took some doing.
One day
I noticed some giddiness
Present between us.
"Oh, no," I thought,
Passing it off to
Something I drank.
Then, one morning
I rolled over and asked,
When did my heart
Break open to this world?
And How
Can I Fit
Everyone
Into the
Church?

Under the Mattress

If you are wearing
A crown
Whose sky gives
Birth
To the whole world-
You know
How to create
Song and kings and queens.

The stonemasons and maids among us
Have no less space in that
Pregnant forest of the heart.

If you have not moved into yours yet,
What good are your heavy pockets?
Reach in and pull out your
Garland, cramped and star-filled.

I have hidden mine under the mattress
For eons,
Like a well-worn secret.

Finally, one night
I wandered
Back into the garden
Bidden by the richness of its perfume,
Which I now wear gladly, like a gift.
Its fragrance
Is the scent of light.

I Heard a Whisper

I heard a whisper in the night-
I awoke to no one but the stars to listen to.
Somehow their light broke through the window
And spoke a language
My heart recognized and remembered.

It turned me towards myself again-
Someone I had silenced years ago.

It seems we let strangers into the house, only to turn ourselves
away.

Carrying the soft carcass of our longing
Like a burden- for a later that never comes.
Or listening with no holiness in our ears.

It causes the wild and magnificent
Pinions of our lives
To fold into an empty field,
Rendering us earthbound
And strangely disconnected to the conversant sky.

Now
Like an infant in your arms,
Open the closed envelope
And read the invitation you crafted so long ago:
An ancient verse calling you back to yourself.

Cradle the parched spoken and unspoken words
Like a template.

Listen.
Can you hear it?

The sky has opened up again,
Into a raucous symphony of sound-
Happy that the part of you
Knocking at the door for re-admittance,
Clothed in forgotten light
Has come home.

At the Threshold

There is an open door
Somewhere in the universe—
Perpetually calling us to
Journey closer to the sound of beauty.

Inviting all the tears we feel
About loss and ugliness
To cascade on the floor beneath us;
Like a great sadness loosened.

Like remnants leading us to a mysterious threshold…
One that we rarely think about crossing over

Too big, too small, no time,
And then we wonder why
We feel cramped and silent.

If that doorway which calls us
Could entice us through,
Perhaps
We would find
A prayer, like a symphony
In our voice—
Slipping from us like praise—
Emerging from us, like the
Sound
Of a single sigh
For all that beauty
Which we have
Walked into
And
Become.

Finely-Tuned Instruments

Nowhere in my world now
Does the heart say one thing
And the body another—
Like finely- tuned instruments,
They have strung themselves together.
Like voices that have not gotten along
Who have suddenly
Fallen in love
And begun bringing
Each other presents
Hoping to be the first
To give them away
To the other.

Ancient Ribbons

I do not know how to begin.
I do not know how to earn a closeness with you, God.
I feel your presence at my heels,
Where my feet collide with the earth.
I hear your breath mix with mine,
As my mouth learns to form words and sing.
But,
This conflict I see in man…
This relentless gallop, we find ourselves in–
Moving in the confines
Of a dry, lifeless corral—

Somehow my feet and mind
Have known all along
The path that leads to Your door.
Somewhere the hooves of wild happiness,
Groomed and at attention,
Have been ready all along to take us there.
If only we would turn and see them in the open fields,
And, like ancient ribbons tied to a tail,
Follow.

Building a Shrine

My life so far
Has been like
Trying to put a very large love
Through a pinhole.
I have tried to make myself
Small enough to fit into this world.
But finally the shell has rent in two,
And the shrine of my being has emerged.

We are guided home on an invisible thread—
One day the distance between ourselves and the hole
Simply disappears.

And then the love fits perfectly.

There is so much work to do in this world—
When we could simply choose
To be estastically happy.
To take rocks and driftwood and build an altar
To all that is good inside of us,
And to set our one shining life
On fire.

I am

I am a gatekeeper.
I am an entrance point.
I am a huge water-filled urn
Reflecting power

Back into the world.
I am the gray-blue mountains
Joyfully sitting among members of the landscape.
I am a spring green tendril feeling with delight

The roots beneath me.
I am a lightning rod anchoring wildness
From the summer sky.
I remember all of this now,

Like a gift.
Like visiting an ancient stone cairn
And remembering helping to build it.
Like weeping into my hands

And knowing
That I have found my place
In the great circle
Of things.

Tracey Schmidt, a photographer and poet, is a resident of Asheville, NC. Her moving photographs of Native Americans are in a nationally touring museum exhibit, *The Awakening of Turtle Island: Portraits of Native Americans*. This multi-media exhibit won the Regional Designation Award in the Humanities for the Olympics in 1996; more of her work can be seen at: www.traceyschmidt.com.

She teaches creativity and poetry and has taught at such facilities as the North Carolina Center for the Advancement of Teaching, Julia Cameron's Creativity Camp in Taos, NM, and Warren Wilson's Environmental Leadership's Retreat in the Georgian Bay, Canada.

She lives with her black manx, two hives of bees, and three white turtle doves. She has fallen in love with the world. She is still not sure how it happened.